ALL FOR FALL

By Ethel and Leonard Kessler

Parents' Magazine Press / New York

Kenneth Neil
Jason

LIBRARY OF CONGRESS CATALOGING IN PUBLICATION DATA
Kessler, Ethel.
  All for fall.
  SUMMARY: Brief verses explore the colors and
activities of fall.
    1. Autumn—Juvenile poetry. [1. Autumn—Poetry]
I. Kessler, Leonard P., joint author.
II. Title.
PZ8.3.K44Al   811′ .5′ 4   74-2249
ISBN 0-8193-0735-1 ISBN 0-8193-0736-X (lib. bdg.)

For Lili Kessler
who paints the wonderful colors of fall

The colors of winter
are cold and dull.
The colors of summer
are golden bright.
The colors of spring
are fresh and wet.
But what are the colors
of fall?

Green is the color
of early fall.
Green grass,
green fields,
green trees...

yellow green,

bright green,

dark green,

light green,

blue green,

gray green.

Listen at night...
Katy-did, katy-did
katy-did, katy-did
katy-didn't, katy-did.
Leafy green katydids
fiddle their songs.

In the misty autumn mornings
the birds are quiet.
They no longer sing
their cheery songs.

Fall time is school time.
It's early go to bed time.
It's wake up sleepyhead time,
you'll miss that yellow bus.
Wait! Wait! Wait for us!

Fall is yellow.
Yellow goldenrod,
yellow squash.
Sweet yellow corn with melted butter,
just picked in early fall.

Duck bills
yellow.
Duck feet
flat.
In the hazy days of fall
the geese are getting fat.
Fatten up, geese,
it's time for you to go.

Fly away, geese.

Fly away, ducks.

Fly away, summer birds.

Fly, fly, butterflies.

Fly away in the fall.

The apples are
all red and yellow,
ripe and juicy,
ripe and ready.
Now's the time
to pick the apples.
Bite an apple,
bake an apple,
make an apple pie.

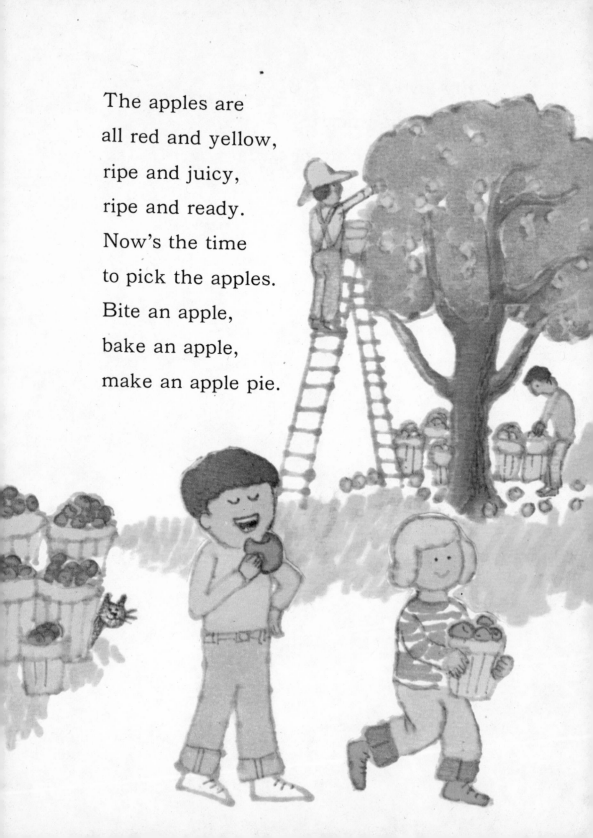

What is purple in the fall?

Purple shadows.

Dahlias tall.

Wheels of asters.

Purple hills.

Purple fingers

from picking purple grapes.

Purple tongue

from eating purple jelly.

Then in early fall
come the nicest days of all —
warm, fair days of Indian summer.
Go out and play.
No sweaters today.

Dewy mornings,

frosty nights.

Day by day

the colors change.

Scarlet, yellow,

crimson, gold.

Reds and purples,

brown and orange.

Patches of color

sunlight bright.

Fall is black

and orange and white.

Orange pumpkins,

plump and round.

Black cats.

Witches' hats.

Black shadows fall.

White ghosts.

Orange twinkling lights

from jack-o'-lanterns

blinking at the black night.

Fall is Halloween.

Fall is brown.
Brown nuts
fat and ready
all fall down.
Brown milkweed seeds
sail in the wind
on silky white parachutes.
Chestnuts drop
from prickly chestnut burrs.

Acorns plop
from oak trees.
Rusty brown chipmunks
scamper around.
Find a seed —
hide a seed.
Find a nut —
hide a nut.

Brown earth,

brown grass.

A lonely bird's nest

empty brown.

Dead leaves

dry and crunchy brown.

Rake them all together

into a great big pile.

1 . . . 2 . . . 3

We all fall

DOWN!

Fall is a gray
November day.
Gray frost
on November trees.
Gray sky.
A sunless day.
Empty logs
wrinkled gray.
One gray feather
on a gray broken branch.
Gray squirrels
and brown leaves.

A sudden cold
November storm.
The gray, wet wind
beats against my windows.
It whips the last frosty leaf
from the gray maple tree.
It bends the tree.
It shakes the twigs.
It breaks the branches
that snap and fall
on the roof.

The last gray days of fall
are the shortest days of all.
Each day ends
with a little less light.
The night darkness
comes early.
A gray squirrel
runs through
the brown leaves.
He's ready for winter.

Down in the ground
fat furry woodchucks
are curled.
They are ready
for the long winter sleep.

The chipmunk is
safe and snug
in his warm little nest.
He is ready.
Deep in the mud
turtle is ready for winter.

Mother and daddy are ready.

I'm ready too.

How about...

Y O U !

Ethel and Leonard Kessler were both educated at Carnegie Tech (now Carnegie Mellon) and both have a continuing interest in children, Ethel as a kindergarten teacher and Leonard through his books, which number over one hundred. More than forty of these he has written as well as illustrated, many with the active participation of his wife, and four of their books have made the Ten Best lists of the *New York Times*.

All for Fall is a sequel to *Splish Splash!* (about spring) and *Slush Slush!* (about winter) published by Parents' Magazine Press.